Disclaimer

This book is an account of actual events, of false accusations of child sexual abuse made against me. I am not a doctor, lawyer, law enforcement officer, psychologist or other trained professional. I am someone who has lived through and been permanently altered by events that unfolded over several years including: being falsely accused, two trials, a divide in my family and living life after being cleared. My purpose in sharing my story is to help other innocent people accused of similar crimes to prepare themselves and their family physically, mentally and emotionally for what is ahead. Child abuse is a horrible crime that destroys lives and families. False accusations can be equally devastating. In this book you will read many of my opinions and interpretations of the events and perceptions about the people in my case. I have changed the names of everyone involved, including myself, to allow me to write openly about the events that occurred without fear of retaliation and to better help other innocent people. This book should only be used as a guide to prepare yourself for what is ahead of you, if you or a loved one have been falsely accused of sexual abuse.

Preface

There are real problems within the system. These problems can affect you and your family. False accusations are very serious. The repercussions are permanent. If you have been falsely accused you need to start working immediately to defend yourself. I want to see all innocent people cleared of the charges against them and all guilty people sent to prison. Unfortunately, that does not always happen. Innocent people do go to jail and you will need to work hard to not be one of them.

I believe my case is an example of extreme abuse of the system. I will show some of the abuses and recount the events I experienced. You will have to determine what applies to your case, so you can disprove the accusations against you with your lawyer in the lead. I will also discuss some of the emotional highs and lows of my experiences. By understanding what is ahead you will be better able to separate the emotional side from the factual side. Learning to do this could be the difference between years in prison and being free to live your life with the people you love.

CHAPTER 1

My Background

As I stated in the preface, I am not a doctor, lawyer, law enforcement officer, psychologist or other trained professional. I am a man who was falsely accused of sexually abusing two young boys who were my nephew's children. I have written this book to share my experience with the legal system and the investigating authorities to help give some insight into how the system works and what you should expect. I speak very candidly about the emotional toll this has taken on my family and me. I want you to be as prepared as possible. My hope is you will find some information from this book useful in your situation so you can fight for your innocence and prevent any major mistakes that could cost you your freedom.

False accusations of child sexual abuse are not limited to any age group, gender, race, social or economic status. No one is immune from the possibility of being falsely accused. The impact is lasting and life changing for everyone involved. In 2005, that's exactly what happened to me when I first learned my in-laws, with whom I thought I had a very good relationship with, believed I had molested their young children. Despite my innocence this would start my life down a difficult path lasting years. It culminated in a judge finding me not-guilty, a permanent division between my family and my wife's relatives, tens of thousands of dollars in legal fees and changes in the way I live my life.

Prior to the accusations I led what I consider a normal life. I am a middle-class blue collar worker. At the time of the accusation I had been married for 28 years with two adult sons and one adult daughter. There is nothing unusual in my life that would lead anyone to believe I would abuse a child.

The problem I had in the beginning, in relationship to the false accusation, was I was not prepared. The emotional, physical and financial stress put on me, my family and my friends was tremendous. I needed to find the strength and courage to face the ordeal. I had two choices. I could stand and fight or I could give up. Giving up is not in my nature although there were moments that tested my strength. Throughout the ordeal you will find yourself and your family experiencing a wide range of intense emotions. You are literally fighting for your life, even if you don't realize it yet. In my darkest moments, I was ready to give up and just do away with myself. During these difficult times I leaned on the love and support of my family and friends to give me the strength to fight and prove my innocence.

You'll need to look at every aspect of your life starting in the beginning. I was born a year after my parents were married. My brother was born eighteen months later. When I was three years old we moved into the house I lived in until a year before I was married. My mother and father are still married and live in my childhood home. We were not rich, my parents worked hard to provide for us. Looking back at my childhood I had a loving home with happy memories of growing up. There was nothing in my upbringing to indicate I would abuse a child.

You also may have had a normal upbringing but you must look deeply into your life for any circumstances that the accusers or prosecutors may try to use against you. Even though you are innocent if an accusation is made there is a good possibility you will end up in court. In court your character, past activities and people you have associated with can come into question. I went to a catholic grade school and high school. I had to consider if there were implications because at the time of my accusation there were many scandals coming out of priest sexual abuse of students from all over the United States. Would a jury perceive my catholic education negatively? Every detail matters.

I met my wife the September after I graduated high school. She was going into her senior year. So her family knew me for a long time. I reviewed the relationship between my wife's family and myself to be sure there was nothing that could implicate or imply that I was capable of abusing a child. My wife's sister was divorced early in her marriage. We babysat her two sons quite often. One of the boys was the father of the children I was accused of abusing.

Because of his mothers divorce the father of the children in question spent two to three days a week at our home growing up. Most times he and his brother stayed overnight. This continued from the time he was in diapers to about fifth or sixth grade. He knew me quite well. He knew what type of person I am and I was sure he knew nothing had happened. From the time my wife and I first heard the accusation in August 2005 to the following February when the police came to my home I had a false sense of security. I truly believed the father knew me so well, he knew I could not commit such an evil act. I was convinced he would intervene and put a stop to all these false allegations.

At this point, I don't really know if someone had tried to convince me how serious this was that I would have believed them. The normal life of most people does not prepare them for an accusation of child abuse and criminal charges. You need to look into your life with an objective eye. Everyone has something in their life that they may not be proud of. You should review every facet of your life honestly, objectively and completely. You need to see if there is anything can be used to build a case against you.

You also need to look into the life of the person making the false accusation. There may be things in their past that may be important to the case. Your lawyer may have to question the character, background, the past or current mental stability of the accuser. Information you gather may help in that effort.

CHAPTER 2

The Accusation is Made

In August of 2005, my wife was confronted by our nephew's wife. She told my wife that she believed I had taken sexually explicit pictures of her sons. The accusation of child sexual abuse is a scarlet letter that will follow you and your family forever. It will have an effect on you and your family's life style, emotions, finances, relationships and much more.

An innocent person will not see an accusation of child abuse coming. Why would you? You are innocent. A false accusation will most likely come primarily from two sources. The first source can be a misunderstanding or misinterpretation from a child's words or actions. It could also be a blatant lie from the child for a variety of reasons. The second source comes from an adult. The accusing adult may have a personal reason to do you harm. They may do it for their own gain or feel the need to seek some perverted sort of revenge. The adult making the accusation could also possibly have a mental disorder or they may have a history of being abused themselves. They may misconstrue something the child says inferring abuse from an innocent statement. You may never know the real reason of the accusation. The reality is it will likely never make sense, looking for reason in an unreasonable situation will only confuse you more. The best thing to do is accept you will never get the answers you are looking for and focus on proving your innocence.

The source of the accusation will not always be clear. My wife and I were led to believe the children were the source of the accusation. It was not until later in the process we began to see a pattern indicating the mother was manipulating and manufacturing the children's statements. When you first become aware of an accusation against you, it is important you take immediate defensive action. If you focus on what you believe is the source of the accusation you could be misled and waste precious time.

When I first heard the allegation from my wife I took it seriously but I did not believe I was in serious trouble. After all, this was my family and I knew I was innocent. We believed it was a simple misunderstanding. We later found out that the oldest child in my case had been going to a child psychologist for three months at the time my wife learned of the accusation. The youngest child had only gone to therapy for a month. The only thing to come out of the sessions with the psychologist was that the oldest child stated someone had taken "bad pictures in a small room next to a big room where you play games and the pictures come out the bottom". The mother inferred the pictures must have been sexual in nature.

As it turned out my wife and her sister (the children's fraternal grandmother) had taken the kids to a seashore town on a previous vacation. They were on the boardwalk and took pictures in a photo booth next to an arcade. The children believed the pictures were bad because they were too small for the camera and only parts of their heads were in the photos. My name was never brought up during the children's therapy sessions. The mother of the children interpreted the child's statement on her own. The mother told my wife she believed the small room was our downstairs powder room and the big room was our basement. The mother interpreted the pictures as "coming from the bottom", as pictures from a Polaroid camera.

Taking the children to a child psychologist was the start of the process. I did not know of the therapy until the mother talked to my wife three months after the children started therapy. During those three months, we had been at their house and nothing was said. They had borrowed our van for their vacation and nothing was said. Looking back, this illustrates many times the process of developing a case against you will start without your knowledge. This will give the advantage to the other side. Even after I did find out about the accusations, the parents would not talk to me. They even blocked our phone calls.

My nephew's wife drawing her own conclusions and expressing her interpretations should have been a big red flag. It was a situation I did not understand at the time. The psychologist did not suspect abuse. However, the mother went against a professional opinion and formed her own opinion. Although I was aware of the accusation, the process continued to escalate without my knowledge. If it is the adult manipulating the accusation they will start to look for allies and convert people to their side against you. Converting people against you will not be as hard as you would think. I am not just talking about your family and friends. I am also talking about the police, district attorneys and social agencies and/or social workers.

Many accusations of child sexual abuse are true. What happens when the accusations are not true? If you are lucky, the professionals involved in your case will have integrity and you will be investigated fairly and objectively. Don't assume investigators are working in your best interest. Their job is to collect evidence against you for prosecution and let the courts decide.

Here is one example of the mentality of the professionals who are working against you. The former District Attorney of my city, who later became a high ranking politician, said in a television interview he would bring cases of sexual abuse to trial even when he knew he didn't have enough evidence to get a conviction. His purpose was to let it be known there was a child predator out there. It didn't occur to him the defendants may be innocent and he was causing them incredible emotional and financial hardship.

Because of the heinous nature of these crimes the system is becoming more and more flawed and skewed in favor of the alleged victim and against the alleged perpetrator. In my opinion, many investigators automatically assume you are guilty and want you convicted at all costs because they view you as a predator. You should listen to an old cliché "Prepare for the worst and hope for the best".

When you first hear someone suspects you of child sexual abuse you will not fully understand the possible consequences. Your first reaction will be shock. You will try to find out what you are accused of doing. You will try to find out when it was supposed to have happened. You will try to find out exactly what the child said and any other facts. Most of all you will proclaim your innocence to everyone. You won't understand the process begins before you are aware of an accusation against you and it will continue without your knowledge. Even when you become aware of the accusation the process will continue. The most important thing to do when an insinuation or accusation is made against you is to seek professional legal help. You need to start setting your defense up from the beginning. You should also be careful who you talk to. Do not talk to a police officer, district attorney, social worker or other investigator without a lawyer.

CHAPTER 3

Meet the Investigators

Now that a case has started to be made against you, you will enter a part of the justice system unlike any other. You will encounter law enforcement officers, district attorneys (DA), child protective services (CPS), investigators, psychologist, therapist, forensic interviewers, etc. Get ready, because many of those people are there to find you guilty. In an age of scientific, technological and medical advances the child protective and law enforcement agencies are moving backward when it comes to the rights of the accused.

There are law enforcement officials, prosecutors and social workers who are capitalizing on the moral panic of child sexual abuse for their own advancement. There is a Noble Cause syndrome where police officers and prosecutors are willing to break the law to get a conviction because they believe they are helping society by looking after the "greater good". There are judges and juries that when in doubt will side with the child. There are the social agencies and social workers with their own issues, problems and agendas.

In my case, the mother called the Department of Human Services (DHS) and the police in January 2006. On that same day the reports were filed, the oldest child was in the police station being interviewed by a forensic interviewer. The interview was observed by a Department of Human Services investigator and a police detective. In later testimony the police officer admitted he had left the observation room after five minutes. The parents were also interviewed by the forensic interviewer and the police. During the police interview both of the parents stated there were no results from their children's sessions with the psychologist. The father confirmed this in court testimony. Despite a professional psychiatric opinion that no abuse had taken place the police proceeded with the investigation.

The Department of Human Services investigator called me two weeks after the parents' and children's interview. The investigator did not tell me the police were involved and the oldest child had been interviewed. I was not aware of the exact allegations against me. When he called I was trying to figure out what was happening and what it meant. I was in a state of shock and confusion. As he questioned me, I tried to explain I was innocent and the children had not been under my care for a long time. It did not matter to him. He was armed with the child's interview. He was not looking for the truth, he was looking for me to say something he could use as evidence against me.

The DHS investigator continued to question me.

The questions confused me even more. The accusations were made in the form of his questions. I had not heard these accusations before. I tried to answer his questions. I believed I could convince him I was innocent. The phone call was not long. My wife had picked up the phone at the same time and was listening in on the call. Shortly into the call my wife broke in and told me to hang up and don't talk to anyone without a lawyer.

In hind sight and based on his reports, the investigator had already made up his mind. If my wife had not told me to hang up I could have given him information that not only the civil authorities would use but the criminal investigators would have used too.

The Department of Human Services investigator is required by law in my state to come to my home to investigate the site of the accusation. He did not come to my home. He had called me before I received a letter from DHS, also required by state law, advising me of my rights. I did not have any further contact with him until eight months after my trail at my expungement hearing.

I still did not get a lawyer and I did not understand the gravity of his call. I was in a state of confusion and I wanted to take a couple of days to digest what had happened and develop a plan. I still believed this misunderstanding could and would be worked out. I based my belief on my innocence. I was at a severe disadvantage because I was not aware of events that had already taken place. If a municipal or county Child Protective Services question you, you can be sure the police are probably not far behind.

Several days after the DHS investigator called me five police officers showed up at my house with a search warrant. They showed up at 5:30 P.M. on a Friday. Again I made the mistake of trying to express my innocence to the police. This could have been a major mistake on my part. Once the police show up, you have to understand you are a suspect. If you think of this objectively, how many suspects tell the police they are innocent? The police do not want to hear your side. If you try to reason with the police you can only harm yourself. If the police were able to get a search warrant they must have probable cause. Because you are innocent you are probably not fully aware of the charges or accusations against you. Even if you are aware, the police are there to search your home not to listen to you plead your case.

They left about 7:30 p.m., nothing was found during the search although my computers and some personal property were seized. Before they left, the police asked me if I could come in for an interview on Monday at 9:30 a.m.,

I agreed. It was not until the day police showed up at my house with a search warrant that I realized I was in legal trouble. It was only then I understood the situation could no longer be handled by a discussion with my nephew's family. Even though I had done nothing wrong I was in serious trouble. I finally realized I needed legal counsel to protect my rights.

When the police left I was able to obtain, though a family friend, a very good lawyer who specializes in defending child abuse charges. I met with the lawyer at 7 p.m. on Saturday night. Monday morning my lawyer called the police officers to confirm the interview at 9:30. Now that I had a lawyer the police had no interest in talking to me and they cancelled the interview.

This could have been the most fatal part of process for me. The police came to my house on Friday. If I had not gotten a lawyer to meet with me the next day, Saturday, I believe I would be in prison now.

One hour with a lawyer will make you aware of the gravity of the situation and the consequences. What I wanted to know most of all was would I be arrested? My lawyer did not know but he did not paint an optimistic picture. I still had a false sense of security until my arrest warrant was issued. The situation becomes more difficult because you are innocent. It is difficult to defend or prepare a defense if you don't know exactly what you are being accused of. The search warrant listed the charges but it did not give specifics. This point in the process can be very frustrating because you are not sure what you are fighting. The one thing you can do to help yourself is to start evaluating your lawyer from the beginning. Your lawyer may be the difference between freedom and years in prison for a crime you did not commit.

In April, 2006 the district attorney issued a warrant for my arrest. The arrest warrant contained five charges of sexual abuse against the oldest child of my nephew. This was one of the lowest days of my life. I was confused and frustrated because I still did not know the specifics of the accusations. My lawyer arranged for me to turn myself in. I spent twenty-six hours in jail. I became even more confused at my bail hearing. The arrest warrant only contained charges related to the oldest child. When I got to the bail hearing I found that I was being charged for both children. Bail was set at $160,000. My lawyer got the bail reduced to $8,000 for each child for a total of $16,000 (another reason for a good lawyer). When I was taken back to a cell after the bail hearing I was moved to a different cell because of the seriousness of the charges. I waited three hours in my new cell with three people charged with murder and one with attempted murder. I had never been in legal trouble my whole life. I wasn't sure what to do. I knew being charged with sexually abusing a child did not make you safe in jail. I was so scared that when my cellmates asked what I had done I told them I was in a fight and I had severely injured someone. My wife and my brother bailed me out of jail. A date for my preliminary hearing was set at my bail hearing.

CHAPTER 4

You Are Now Entering the System

The phrase "best interest of the child" is often used by social, civil, police, prosecutorial and judicial entities or the individuals employed by these agencies. The problem with this phrase is it can be used to deprive an individual of their legal and civil rights. The best interest of the child is used as an overreaching justification for a variety of injustices. It should be the best interest of all the parties. When authorities use this phrase to err on siding with the child it makes it difficult to get a fair trial.

When a social worker sends a child to therapy before abuse has been confirmed they are not acting in the "best interest of the child". When a police investigator takes the word of an accusing caregiver without investigating the facts, without checking the background of all parties involved or without objectively listening to both sides they are not acting in the "best interest of the child". When a prosecutor decides to proceed with a case despite not having enough evidence, they have permanently scared the child and they have not acted in the "best interest of the child". These things happen everyday in many jurisdictions throughout the world. There are also many more abuses of the system. You have to be aware of the people involved in the investigation and the roles they play.

Many times social agencies or social workers are the first point of contact in a child sexual abuse case. The social worker is usually employed by a municipal child protective services (CPS) agency or a child advocacy center (CAC). Almost all social workers start their careers with the best intentions. Along the way though, they can be influenced by many factors. They can be influenced by previous cases. They can be pressured by police, prosecutors, their peers or the accusing caregiver. Their first contact is almost always the child and the accusing caregiver and they can form an opinion before they ever talk to you or meet you.

The investigator for the county or municipal child protective services has enormous power over your situation. Based on their investigation, you can be placed on your local and/or state child protective lists. In my case, a call was received from the mother of the children by the local child protective hotline. The investigator was assigned to my case. He listened to an interview of the oldest child conducted by a forensic interviewer. He then talked to me on the phone for two or three minutes. Based on these actions he found the complaint against me substantiated. This immediately placed me on the child protective list which was searchable by the public via the internet. That is not a misprint, in the United States your name can and will likely be put on a child protective list before your trial takes place.

The DHS investigator did not interview the parents. He did not observe the interviews of the parents conducted by the forensic interviewer or the police. He did not come to my home to investigate the site of the alleged incident. He did not check the background of anyone involved including me. He did not testify at my trial. Eight months after my trial the investigator was a witness at my expungement hearing. He was questioned by my lawyer as to why he had not filled out the portion of the report that stated what I had done. He nervously tried to make excuses but he could not state what I had done.

In many jurisdictions child protective agencies and their employees are over whelmed and over worked. This is no excuse for incomplete or biased investigations. The future of you and your family is at stake. You have a right to a complete and objective investigation under the law. This does not happen all the time and do not assume it will happen in your case.

Sometimes an accusing caregiver will contact a child advocacy center first or they will be referred to a CAC by social services or the police department. The social workers employed by a child advocacy center may never talk to you or meet with you. In fact, many of the websites of the child advocacy centers state that they do not talk to the accused. They become an advocate for the child and establish a relationship with the accusing caregiver. This can happen even before an investigation has begun or concluded. Child advocacy agencies often offer therapy for the child and the caregiver before an investigation is started or concluded. This is a dangerous and irresponsible policy you may have to deal with. Physical evidence can confirm sexual abuse although it may not confirm the perpetrator and therapy would be appropriate. In the majority of cases there is no physical evidence. In these cases a third party opinion by a licensed psychiatrist or psychologist should be obtained before recommending therapy.

If therapy is started before there is confirmation of child sexual abuse it may corrupt the process. The purpose of therapy is to heal or treat a problem. When you are falsely accused the alleged victim does not have a problem. Therapy becomes a form of brain washing. Imagine putting a cast on a young child's arm and telling the child their arm is broken. If there is a relationship of trust established between the child and the person telling the child their arm is broken the child will believe their arm is broken.

The Child Advocacy Center involved in my case stated on their web site and in their annual report, therapy can be started even before they come into the center. The oldest child's interview began at 4 P.M. and it was conducted by a forensic interviewer from the CAC. According to the police report, their interview of the mother began at 4:07 P.M. During the interview, the police officer conducting the interview told the mother her child would be going to therapy through the child advocacy center. The child's interview was still in progress. The police officer had not seen any of the child's interview and no investigation had taken place. The place the child advocacy center sent the child required sexual abuse to be confirmed before they accepted a client for therapy. The child ended up going to forty-two therapy sessions for something that never happened.

My city uses the multidisciplinary team concept (MDT). This is an experimental concept that combines the District Attorney's Office, the Police Department, Municipal or County Child Protective Services Agency and a Child's Advocacy Center into a single investigating entity. I will discuss this concept later in the book. Because of the MDT concept a forensic interviewer from the child advocacy center was called in. The forensic interviewer interviewed the parents and the child.

It is important to understand the accusing caregiver may be the one that is manufacturing or manipulating the facts and/or the child's statements. In my case, the forensic interviewer interviewed the parents first, then she interviewed the oldest child. The police and the DA's Office used this interview as a base for probable cause and for evidence.

Except for one sentence during the parent's interview the mother did all the talking. The mother had a history of drug and alcohol use. She also had a history of suicide attempts and paranoia stemming from sexual abuse of a close family member by a neighbor. None of this mattered to the forensic interviewer. In fact, I filed a civil lawsuit against the MDT at the end of my ordeal. As a response to my lawsuit it was the forensic interviewer's position that it was not her job to investigate or verify any part of the interview of the caregiver or the child. It was also her position that she did not need to check the background of the accusing caregiver or the child, however she did state in her report that the background check on me came up negative (information she got from the police). The forensic interviewer also stated in her response to my civil suit that it was not her job to talk to me. It was also not her responsibility to confirm any information obtained. A federal judge agreed with her and dismissed my civil lawsuit against her.

You can see building a case against you can be quite one sided. In fact, when building a case against you the credibility of the accusers will probably not be checked. Most likely the first person to question the credibility of the parties involved will be your lawyer. If the police do the first interview the outcome will most likely be the same.

CHAPTER 5

A Deeper Look at the System

There is a criminal and civil side to the system. You will have to deal with both sides. In your immediate future the criminal side is more important because it is the one that can send you to prison. The civil investigation findings can be used on the criminal side and the criminal investigation findings can be used on the civil side. So from the beginning you have two forces working against you. I would like to preface this chapter by saying there are many honest and objective investigators. Through the investigative process several people will have input and influence during the course of the investigation. There is a good chance someone involved will misinterpret, manipulate, manufacture or simply be convinced something happened. Because there is a child involved the attitude will often be "why take a chance". That could be enough to send you to trial.

A child abuse investigation is unlike any other. The police do not need any physical evidence. In most cases there is not any evidence in the beginning except the word of an accusing adult or child. Since you are innocent there is no direct evidence but there may be circumstantial or even fabricated evidence. You may become optimistic because you will think the police or any other investigator is not going to find anything. Don't let this fool you. We have all seen movies and TV shows where the police work feverishly to build a case. In almost all criminal investigations it is true the police need to build a case but when it comes to a child abuse case the police need to make a case. This is because many times it comes down to one person's word against another person's word.

Let me give you a hypothetical example. A mother and father are separated. While staying with the father a five year old boy has an accident and goes to the bathroom in his pants. The father cleans up the mess and gives the child a bath. He washes the child's butt, takes him out of the bath, dries him off and gets him dressed. The incident is forgotten and they move on with their day. When the child returns to the mother it somehow comes out that the father touched the child's butt. When the mother hears this she becomes alarmed. The mother can be a vindictive person, she can have mental problems or she can simply be overly cautious. The mother goes and reports the incident to the police. When the police interview the young boy he is embarrassed to tell the accident part of the story and he only tells the bath part of the story.

The police now have probable cause. Social services will be contacted. The child will probably be sent to therapy and the police will talk to the DA about a search warrant. In my case, and in many of the cases that I have read, the police do not really have an interest in talking to the alleged perpetrator. Most likely the father will have no idea that all of this is going on until the police show up at his door. In this example I used a separated mother and father, but it can be grandparents, an aunt or uncle, a friend, a babysitter, etc.

CHAPTER 6

Confirmatory Bias

In the previous example, the mother and the child are the only ones who have talked to the police and/or a social worker. The child may have also been interviewed by a forensic interviewer. Many times the parties involved will believe the story of the mother and child. An investigator or interviewer should not form an opinion on whether or not abuse has taken place until all the facts have been gathered and all parties have been interviewed and investigated. I am very skeptical of the protocols and procedures used in child abuse cases so I looked up "confirmatory bias" in the skeptic's   dictionary http://www.skepdic.com/confirmbias.html. I encourage you to the same for your own understanding. In summary, this is what it said as of December 2011.

Confirmatory Bias is the selective thinking of looking for evidence that supports your opinion and discarding evidence that disproves your opinion. Basically, investigators see information from a viewpoint of how it proves you are guilty. They will not see the possibilities of how you are innocent.

It is my opinion that confirmatory bias should be a

criminal offense. If an innocent child is convinced they have been sexually abused they will suffer the same mental scars as a child who has been abused. One State District Attorney's report from 2006 stated that out of 4,000 child sexual abuse cases a year 160 of the victims will become hardened criminals as a result of abuse. Other studies show that up to 50% of child abuse cases are committed by people who have been abused as a child. The people brainwashing innocent children as a result of confirmatory bias should be held responsible. Instead, as I found out in my civil lawsuit, they are protected by the federal court.

Before I go into the dangers of confirmatory bias there is a positive side. The police, social workers, district attorneys, etc involved in investigation or fact finding in your case will make mistakes if they suffer from confirmatory bias. The odds are that the professionals involved will have some sort of confirmatory bias. Because they believe something happened they will miss steps and make errors. Since you are innocent you might assume proper procedures and protocols will be followed that will show the truth. This is not true. Confirmatory bias, improper training and many other reasons will contribute to mistakes being made by investigators and fact finders. The difference is mistakes made because of confirmatory bias are intentional.

You have to track and review all documentation and actions taken in your case. You may have a great lawyer. But your lawyer will not know personal information. You will see things in reports and interviews that may be wrong or missing. Don't count on your lawyer picking up these things. It is not good enough to know something is wrong or missing. You will have to prove it. Remember you are dealing with investigators who think you are guilty. The information you gather will probably have to be used at your preliminary hearing, criminal trial, civil trial and/or expungment hearing.

Most of the intentional mistakes are made because information is missing. Investigators and fact finders will look to increase, manufacture or manipulate information or statements that strengthen the case of child sexual abuse against you. There is no objectivity and many times there is an absence of professionalism. In fact, information that may show your innocence may be hidden or ignored. In my case, the investigating officer admitted on the witness stand that the only investigation the police had done was the interview of the child. The mother in my case brought a drawing that was allegedly drawn by the oldest child at home. The child also drew a picture during his interview. Both drawings were kept in the forensic interviewers files at her CAC's office. She even stated that in her report. The drawings were concealed from my attorney and me until two days before my scheduled trial date. The police and the district attorney's office knew these drawings were to be used as evidence yet they allowed them to be hidden in the CAC's files.

Here are some of the common mistakes made by investigators and fact finders because of confirmatory bias: <u>Mistakes in documentation, reports and/or correspondence.</u> In my case there were many errors. The officer who filled out the search warrant stated that he had witnessed the child's interview. The documentation showed that he was interviewing the mother at the same time as the child's interview. So it was impossible for him to observe the child's interview since they were occurring simultaneously. Also on the forensic interviewer's report the officer was not listed as an observer. Because of this information my lawyer and I had a discussion as to whether to fight the validity of the search warrant. We decided that since nothing was found it was better to allow the warrant to stand.

The other police officer involved in my case, a detective, wrote the arrest warrant. The first part of the arrest warrant was copied and pasted from the search warrant. Since the first officer did not observe the interview I looked to see if the detective had observed the interview.

In the police report I found that the detective was interviewing the mother along with his partner at the same time as the child's interview.

The detective also listed a camera on the arrest warrant as being seized during the search warrant. I told the police it was a new camera. The parents of the children stated I had not been alone with their children since February of 2005. The camera the police seized was not available for sale until August of 2005. Because of confirmatory bias the police did not investigate my claim.

The statements attributed to the child in various reports and warrants did not match or were not in the forensic interview of the child. Because of confirmatory bias the police will manipulate or manufacture evidence. The interview will be used as a base for probable cause or as evidence. The intentional mistakes made here will be the police taking statements out of context, changing a statement to make you look guilty or adding to a child's statement. In some cases they will take statements from others and attribute them to the child. For example, on my arrest warrant the last paragraph was a statement the police said was made by the child. It was a direct quote made by the mother on the police report. The police just copied it from their report of the mother's interview and claimed the child made the statement.

Do not accept any documentation or reports at face

value. You have to become an investigator. What is not in a document or report may be as important as what is in there. In the forensic interview report the interviewer asked the child if it is okay to lie. The child replied "no unless it was an accident". That statement was never followed up on and it indicated the child thought it was ok to lie as long as they said it was an accident later. This makes all of his statements questionable.

In the parents interviews with the police they were never even asked if they were married and lived in the same house. The parents were never asked when they thought the incident happened. My computers were seized in the search of my home. In an investigative report there was one line that stated "secret service report on computers negative". I never received a copy of that report because it would have helped my defense.

During the course of the oldest child's interview, the forensic interviewer took three breaks to talk to the team. There was no documentation of the discussions during the breaks. The mother was present at the team discussion during the breaks and I believe she must have had an influence on what is supposed to be an objective interview. In my case there is absolutely no documentation of the police talking to the children. They must have talked to them before and after the interview. But there was no documentation of that because of confirmatory bias investigators and fact finders will skip steps because they assume guilt. You have to look for what is missing, see how it influences your case and see if can be used in your defense.

Most of the intentional mistakes are made because information is missing. Investigators and fact finders will look to increase, manufacture or manipulate information or statements that strengthen the case of sexual abuse against you. There is no objectivity. In fact, information that may show your innocence may be hidden or ignored. In my case the investigating officer admitted on the witness stand that the only investigation the police had done was the interview of the oldest child. The youngest child was interviewed three weeks after the oldest child. Another police officer was listed as the observer of that interview.

There was no police report on that interview and the officer who was supposed to have observed the second interview was not on the witness list at my trial. Investigators need to check and confirm statements and reports. In my case, both parents told the police that the children had been to a psychologist and there were no results. There was never a report that the police followed up on that information. Both officers involved in my case did not observe the interview: Observing the child's interview is important so the police can observe the intangibles of the interview such as the tone of the questions, body language, etc.

Police can easily manipulate the situation using information you are not aware of. You may also say something new the police may use against you. When there is no objectivity and no professionalism involved in the investigation, you cannot help your case by talking to the police.

When confirmatory bias is involved the police will not look for witnesses or circumstances that will prove your innocence. Including me, five people lived in my house. The back door was never locked and my children and their friends were constantly coming and going through the basement where the abuse allegedly took place. The police never questioned anyone in my house. The police did not even ask who lived in the house. The police did not ask what my occupation was. They did not ask about my work schedule. They did not ask if I was home when the alleged incident happened. The police violated my due process rights by never giving me a time frame when the alleged incident happened. At my trial when the court crier announced everyone stand up for the judge's entrance the assistant DA handed my lawyer a paper with the time frame of when they believed the abuse took place.

Between work and the social organizations I was involved with, I had interacted with hundreds of people on a regular basis. Not one of those people was ever questioned. The law states that you are innocent until proven guilty. You have a right to a fair and objective investigation. If police suffer from confirmatory bias you will not get a fair and objective investigation. In fact, the police will probably enhance or invent events and statements to prove your guilt. The situation is out of your control. You will not know the direction of the investigation or the motivation of the police. When the police came to my home to serve the search warrant they kept saying why would the children lie? My thought was I don't even know what the children had said. However, I do know children often lie for many reasons including: to avoid getting in trouble, attention, or simply because they do not understand right and wrong among many other reasons. I should have understood it at the time. The police statements indicated they believed the children without any response from me and before they had done any investigation.

You will be in a difficult situation when it comes to the investigation. You will not know what the police are thinking or the direction they are taking with the investigation. You will not know critical information. You may have a fair and objective police investigator in your jurisdiction. In these cases, being honest and open may help you avoid arrest and trial. In many cases however, the statements you make can and will be used against you or your statements will be ignored. One good test is to see if the investigator talks to you with your lawyer present. There is only one reason for a police officer or district attorney not to talk to you when you have a lawyer. They are looking for guilt not innocence. The police had already made up their mind I was guilty and they would not speak to me with my lawyer present. Do not take a chance. Get a lawyer and find out all the facts before you say or do anything.

Since United States law states you are innocent until proven guilty investigators and fact finders, in my opinion, have an obligation to seek alternative explanations of the accusation. During the course of my research I found only one state that required background checks on all parties. But even a background check may not reveal relevant facts needed to prove your innocence. There are many factors that may influence the accusing adult. Divorce, child custody, money, drugs, alcohol, revenge, previous sexual abuse and mental problems are some of the most common reasons for someone to fabricate a false accusation against you. These are not uncommon situations or events in today's society yet investigators and fact finders continually ignore these possibilities as an alternative explanation an accusation is not true.

Accusing adults can have several situations that should be investigated. Prior to being falsely accused I overlooked the problems in my own family. The mother in my case did abuse drugs. She was an alcoholic. She had suicide attempts and a close relative who was sexually abused. My wife became ill so our normal habits of visiting them and babysitting changed. We had also regularly given them money to help them financially. When our situation changed and we weren't able to help them financially anymore it may have given them a motive for revenge or delusions of why the normal routine changed. I looked up the warning signs for borderline personality disorder and of the 12 warning signs she had eleven of them. I told the police about all of these things when they searched my home. The police didn't want to hear anything. There was not one question about the mother's life style or past from the police or the forensic interviewer. Had investigators had bothered looking at these issues the credibility of the people against me could have been questioned and my case may have not ever made it to trial. Unfortunately, that isn't the way the system works.

The family life of the caregivers and the children should be examined too. In my situation both parents drank excessively. The mother abused drugs. The maternal grandparents lived on the same street and they were both alcoholics. The aunt of the children lived on the same street and she abused drugs. The children have their own TV in their basement and there were no blocked channels to prevent them from watching adult content. The father kept copies of playboy magazine in the only bathroom in the house. The children's fraternal uncle dealt drugs. The children's fraternal grandfather was convicted of exposing himself. This is a family life that should have raised questions.

Even if you discover questions about the credibility of your accusers it may not matter. First you have to prove the accusing adult's problem exists. Then you will have to show that it has an effect on your case. You certainly won't get any cooperation from the accusing adult. If the authorities suffer from confirmatory bias they probably won't help you either. Don't be deterred. At the very least you can use the information to attack the credibility of the accusing adult if they testify against you at trial.

CHAPTER 7

The Multidisciplinary Team (MDT)

The Multidisciplinary Team concept is gaining acceptance throughout the United States. Many states and jurisdictions have mandated or regulated these teams. It brings together agencies and departments that are involved in the prosecution, investigation and treatment of child sexual abuse. The four main components of the team are usually the District Attorney's Office, the police, the municipal or county child protective services and a child advocacy center. Medical or psychological professionals may also be a part of the team. A forensic interviewer may be hired or one of the agencies or departments may have a forensic interviewer on staff.

There are two main reasons for the formation of a multidisciplinary team. The first is to pool resources and information. The second reason is to try to reduce trauma to the alleged victim by eliminating multiple interviews. In theory, the team concept is a good idea. Sharing information by having the professionals work together should insure the process is fair, objective and complete. If a child is sexually abused it can be very traumatic to relive that memory because of repeated interviews.

The procedures and protocols used by a multidisciplinary team are derived from standards that are tried and tested. They are approved by all the relevant authorities and experts. What the MDT procedures and protocols do not take into account is the human factor. You have people from different agencies and departments working together. The process will be influenced by their personalities, experience, prejudice, opinions, egos, fears, etc. You are innocent. There should be no physical evidence unless the child was abused by someone else. These people will have to make a case based on their opinions and not the facts.

In my case, the child never said I did anything to him before he visited the police station. The MDT was assembled and the child was interviewed. During the interview the child stated he climbed behind the couch. He stated I grabbed him by the butt. If a child climbs behind a couch an easy way to get him is to grab him by the belt and pull him out. The police with their confirmatory bias took the child's statement and said I had done something to his butt. The child also stated that in the kitchen I had chased him with a knife and fork. The police once again using confirmatory bias took this as doing something to the child. In actuality I would cook bacon and eggs for him and I chased him out so he would not get burnt by grease from the bacon pan. The police interpreted the child's statements to created probable cause.

Another danger of the human factor in the MDT is that the police can take statements out of context to create probable cause. In a multidisciplinary team situation the police usually conduct the interview of the child. In my case the officer who filled out the affidavit for the search warrant never saw the interview and the detective who was listed as the observer admitted on the witness stand he left the observation room. In my civil lawsuit I stated that the police officers involved had committed perjury on the search warrant and arrest warrant but the judge ruled this was permissible. The police believe they have immunity and therefore can do what they want to create probable cause.

In my civil suit I stated the forensic interviewer was an actor of the state because she was brought in to do the interview of the child by the police. The judge ruled that she was not an actor of the state. This means that no one bears the responsibility of the interview. The multidisciplinary team can become a shell game. Each person on the team is supposed to have their individual responsibilities but the information gathered can be used by anyone on the team. The investigator from DHS in my case is supposed to come out and inspect the premises. He did not because the police were here for the search warrant. The child drew two pictures that were used as evidence. The police are supposed to hold all evidence but the CAC held the evidence in their files. The police are supposed to observe the interview. They did not. The forensic interviewer is supposed to give the police a report. She did not. In this system, many corners are cut.

I have gone on the internet and researched many multidisciplinary teams throughout the United States. They almost all say the same thing. Their purpose is to share information and protect the victim from the traumatic effect of multiple interviews. This is a recipe for depriving you of your civil rights and finding probable cause so that you can be brought to trial. I want to state before I go on that there are many honest and objective professionals in the MDT's throughout the country. But even objective information can be turned and used against you.

The MDT is supposed to meet regularly to review cases. What happens in those meetings is usually not in the official record. You will not receive minutes of those meetings in discovery. The personalities involved in those meetings can be important too. I watched a movie several times during my ordeal called "Snap Decision". In the movie a widowed mother has her children taken away because of some questionable photos. The investigator from child protective service recommends the children be returned and she states that she believes nothing has happened. The children are returned and the mother thinks that everything is alright. Soon after the police show up at her front door with an arrest warrant. While this is not a MDT situation, it does show that because one agency says one thing it does not mean that other agencies will not form their own opinion and act against you.

Another problem with the multidisciplinary team concept is the results do not depend on first-hand information. This can lead to errors, omissions or misinterpretations in information or documentation. In my case, the police report did not match the interview report. The DHS report did not match the interview report or the police report. The search warrant and arrest warrant did not match any report. When I say match, I mean statements time, places, people involved, etc. were contradictory. The truth will be consistent. Since you are innocent the reports saying you are guilty are not true. When you go to trial inconsistencies in the reports and testimony of experts can cause reasonable doubt.

It is my belief that this is an area you should heavily investigate. The forensic interview report in my case stated the child was susceptible to suggestibility. The police and DHS did not take this into account because to the best of my knowledge they did not receive a copy of the report.

A forensic interviewer is usually used in a MDT situation. They may be highly trained in interview techniques and protocols but that does not mean that their report will be processed correctly. You do not know if there are any interviews of the child prior to the forensic interview. During any interview with a child there are always responses that require follow up. But the purpose of the MDT is to eliminate interviews. In my civil lawsuit the lawyer for the forensic interviewer stated several things. The lawyer stated the interviewer was only responsible for the interview. She did not need to find out any information about me or my family. She did not need any background information on the child or his family. She only needed to form an opinion on the interview itself. It was the job of the police to investigate and confirm information and she did not need to review the police report before she formed her opinion. The federal judge upheld these statements.

The interview in my case was not videotaped. If it is video or audio taped in your case, there are questions about the process that should be asked. The first question should be, are there breaks in the tape. There are a lot of things that can happen during a break in an interview that can contaminant the interview. If the audio or video tape is the only interview used as evidence this raises questions too. A child can easily be coached or intimidated for a one time interview. A tape will also give you the opportunity to review the protocols used. You need to find out what protocols the interviewer is supposed to be using and be sure they are followed. You need to look for leading questions. An audio or video tape may seem devastating to you. Your lawyer should know what to do about a tape but don't leave it all to the lawyer. You know your circumstances. Break the tape down, find out what is not true and see how you can prove it.

In a MDT situation the forensic interview is usually the primary evidence used against you. This gives you several opportunities. The first is you will be able to see if there is a misunderstanding of what the child is saying. In my case, I thought this all started from the child talking about bad pictures. I believed it was a misunderstanding that could be easily cleared up. I received the interview report in discovery after my preliminary hearing. I was shocked when I read the report. The report had some statements from the child that looked bad for me. It had other statements that could be easily explained. The report also had some statements from the child that were not true and could be tracked back to an adult. For example the child stated that something happened in August at 2 A.M. in the morning. It is extremely usual if not impossible for a 4 ½ year old to be able to conceptualize dates and times so specifically let alone recall them a year later. I knew I was innocent so there had to be an alternative explanation for the bad statements. I looked at the mother's interview and I found many of her statements matched the child's statements. With this information I now believed I knew the source of the allegations. It wasn't the children, it was the mother.

On the surface the child is the source of the allegations. You should look carefully at their statement to see if it is possible for the child to have fabricated the story on their own. The child may be a pathological liar or may want to seek some sort of revenge against you. They may be just seeking attention. It is reasonable to believe that the younger the child the less likely they have fabricated the story on their own. Once you have eliminated the child fabricating the allegations you have to look for alternative sources.

In my case, the mother now had the members of the MDT working for her. She had two police officers, two assistant district attorneys, one investigator from DHS, one forensic interviewer form the CAC and her supervisor and one intake coordinator from the CAC all working with her, to find me guilty.

The Multidisciplinary Team can become a maze of information. Much of that information can be mishandled or lost. You have to remember the MDT is formed to protect the child. You may never even meet most of the team members. There will almost always be at least one or two team members that believe you are guilty. The authority or influence they have on the team can determine the course of the process. You will have to sort through the information and reports to see how a case is being developed. You are innocent so there has to be flaws in the case. It will not be easy to find the flaws. Many times it may come down to your word against another person's word. They may be a professional and/or a part of this MDT. Most of the time, your explanation or theories on your case will not be heard or considered until you get to court. When you do get to court you better have your proof ready because you are going up against a team of professionals. Do not count on the truth prevailing simply because you are innocent.

The human factor in a multidisciplinary team effort can be dangerous on levels you may not even think of. In my case, the forensic interviewer was a young girl with a month of experience in interviewing by herself. The two police officers involved were middle aged men. This lends itself to several possibilities. Could two experienced officers influence or intimidate a young girl? Do two experienced officers resent a young girl coming in and facilitating the investigation? In my city, I heard two defense attorneys refer to the division of the assistant DA's office in charge of prosecuting child abuse cases as fanatical. Do you have a person or agency involved in your case that is fanatical about child sexual abuse and punishing perpetrators? There is a host of possibilities you will probably never know. It does not matter if you know. What matters is you continue to look for mistakes. The more fanatical a person is the more likely they are to make errors.

The sharing of information and the mixing of personalities in an MDT can lead to mistakes, intentional manipulation of the facts or fabrication of the facts. Here is a basic outline of some things to look for not only when a MDT is involved but in all cases:

- Are the procedures objective and ethical?
- Are the procedures and protocols appropriate and proper?
- Are all the statements, interviews, reports correct?
- Are statements, interviews, reports complete?
- Are there follow ups on statements, interviews, reports?
- Have social environments and psychological

problems been investigated?

- Have medical and/or psychological professionals been consulted?

- Are statements from witnesses missing or ignored?

- Has the time and circumstances of the accusation been established?

- Have other possibilities been considered by the authorities?

- Is there any physical evidence?

- Have the backgrounds of all parties involved been investigated?

CHAPTER 8

Dealing with and Understanding Your Emotions

When an accusation of sexual abuse is made against you it is the beginning of a whirlwind of emotions. You have to prepare to deal with your feelings and to control your emotions. When you finally understand the consequences of the accusation you will be in almost a constant state of fear and stress. How you deal with your feelings and emotions is up to you. It is in your best interest to maintain control and focus on clearing yourself of these accusations.

When I first heard about the accusation that I had committed sexual abuse, I experienced a wide range of emotions. My first reply was, "What" (DISBELIEF). "Why would they say that", (CONFUSION). "I can't believe they would say that", (SHOCK). This rush of emotions took about 15 seconds. After that because I was innocent I went into denial.

Those emotions will stay with you through the whole process and as time goes on you will experience additional feelings of fear, stress, pain, shame, guilt, anger, hatred, depression and disgust. The feelings you want to avoid are confidence and optimism. Remember the movie "The Fugitive". Harrison Ford (falsely accused of murdering his wife) was in a tunnel running from authorities. He was being chased by Tommy Lee Jones (the Special Agent). Ford turns to Jones and says, "I didn't do it". Tommy Lee Jones reply was, "I don't care". Harrison Ford then jumps out of the tunnel, off the dam and gets away to begin his own investigation. If you become over confident and optimistic that this will go away because you are innocent, and if you believe or trust the people involved in the investigation care about you, you will be spending many years in prison.

I experienced a wide range of emotions during my ordeal. Many of those feelings were so personal I kept them to myself which made it more difficult. What I could share with my family sometimes made it more difficult for them. I spent many sleepless nights trying to deal with and rationalize my situation. The daytime was difficult because of everyday experiences that reminded me of what my family and my life meant to me and what I could lose.

Seeing a person I knew was a tense experience because I wondered what they may have heard and what they thought. Just about everything I did was influenced because of the accusation of child sexual abuse.

Even though you are innocent you still have the accusation hanging over you. It can be a real feeling of helplessness. I was in a department store with my wife. I saw two small children who had lost their mother. I could also see the mother across the store looking for her children. I wanted to help but I did not know if I should get involved. I eventually found a store employee and pointed out the situation. I then quickly headed out of the store. Despite being innocent your actions, feeling and emotions will be affected by the accusation.

I also felt the emotions of my family. Your family will also suffer the emotional stress and pain of the accusation. My wife had to deal with the possibility of life without me. My children would have to live without a father. My oldest son worried I would never see my grandchildren. If you are found guilty of child sexual abuse you will not receive a death sentence. But it will be a death sentence to the family. The accusation of child sexual abuse will change the lives of you and your family. Being found guilty will end life as you and your family know it. The emotional pressure of the possible outcomes will cause pain and stress for you as well as your family. You have to understand your family will be hurting too.

In my case I believed that a guilty verdict was a death sentence. I have heard being convicted of a child sexual abuse crime made it very unsafe for a person in prison. The father of the children in my case was a police officer. I believed being convicted of child sex crime of a police officer's son was a death sentence. I thought within a year of going to prison I would mysteriously die or be killed. My hatred of the children's family and my fear intensified as time went on. In fact my hatred is even stronger today.

Instead of focusing on the hatred I used the energy to focus on my case. Some people can focus on a goal while others are distracted on negative issues. Be the person that can focus on the goal of winning your case and don't be distracted by your feelings and emotions.

POSITIVE TRUST: You cannot make it though this ordeal without moral support. You need to establish a circle of trust. The reason for this is to get past proclaiming your innocence and getting to work proving your innocence. The people in the circle of trust must believe beyond a doubt in your innocence. Somewhere along the way you will start to receive statements and reports. Some of this information will not look or sound good. You will need people who can help you breakdown and analyze the information.

There will be some disappointments when establishing a circle of trust. Most cases involve family members or friends. The accusation of sexual abuse forces people to take sides and form opinions. There will also be those who will say why take a chance. This is a time when you will find out who loves you and who believes in you.

NEGATIVE TRUST: The most important advice I

want to give you is "Get a Good Lawyer". By now I hope you understand you cannot trust social workers, police officers and assistant district attorneys to find the truth. Their job is to gather facts.

Remember this, social workers, police and Assistant DA's are not your friends. Their training, protocols and motivation can come into question when it comes to interpreting the facts. Police officers will do what they have to in order to gather information. Your first instinct may be to trust the police and try to explain your side. That is a mistake. There is a reason the police have to read you your Miranda rights before they arrest you. Up to the point of an arrest the police will use information you give to them no matter how they obtain it. Protect yourself; do not talk to the police without a lawyer.

If you and/or your lawyer are dealing with a district attorney the accusations have probably escalated into some sort of charges against you. The DA's job is to prosecute. Since you are innocent the case against you is probably based on a misinterpretation, manipulation and/or manufacturing of the facts. Your lawyer will be in a better position to deal with the district attorney or to evaluate the DA's position. Do not trust yourself to deal with the DA. You do not know their policy or attitudes in regards to child sexual abuse. Never talk to anyone without a lawyer present.

Disbelief: Child sexual abuse is a horrible crime. Falsely accusing someone of child sexual abuse is an equally horrible crime. The falsely accused is a victim that is treated like a criminal and will suffer emotional anguish, financial hardships and possibly physical illness. Many people falsely accused are solid citizens. They have not been involved in the criminal system. What makes it worse is you may know the person you are accused of abusing.

The initial feeling of disbelief stays with you through the whole process. Even though I was prepared for my preliminary hearing and trial I still couldn't believe it was happening to me. The biggest feeling of disbelief was when the judge at my trial told me to stand up for his decision. I was one of the lucky ones. The judge found me not guilty. I don't want anyone who is innocent to have the feeling of disbelief because they are found guilty.

Confusion: Your confusion will begin with the accusation. A common false accusation comes from a vindictive spouse in a divorce or custody battle. It can also be a simple misunderstanding. It can come from an angry child. It can come from a parent with a mental disorder. It can be used by a caregiver or child as a means of getting attention. The actual source of the charge is not always obvious. If a parent or social worker can coach a child to say they were abused the police and the DA will side with the child. This will add to your confusion because when more people get involved it becomes more difficult to sort out the situation.

An innocent person will never fully understand why they are being accused of sexual abuse. You will go through the whole process asking yourself "why". The reason you are so confused is that you are dealing with pure evil and in the case of a mental disorder you are dealing with crazy. I don't know anyone who can explain evil or crazy people. The consequences of being accused or charged with child sexual abuse are devastating to you, the child, your family and friends. When someone manufactures or manipulates facts and evidence against you they are not only hurting you but a host of other people including the child. You will never figure out evil and/or crazy.

Denial: When you first hear the accusation against you, your first reaction will be to deny that it happened. This is a natural reaction because you didn't do anything wrong. Just because you deny any wrong doing doesn't mean that others will believe you. What may be worse is that others such as social workers or police officers may say they believe you when they really do not. You can deny the act your entire life but you cannot deny the accusation. The sooner you separate the accusation from the act you are being accused of, the faster you will get to work on proving your innocence. Because you are innocent the whole thing will seem unreal to you and it will be easy to deny the reality of the situation. The accusation is real and some awful things can happen to you as a result of that accusation.

The denial comes in the form of ignoring the situation. When I first heard the accusation against me I denied it. I knew I was innocent. Looking back I denied there were other forces at work. Almost immediately I recognized the fact that the mother was involved. Although I knew the mother had issues I denied the possibility she was an evil and crazy person willing to go the distance. I also denied that the father (my nephew), would allow this to continue. I had helped raise him, he knew me as well as any son knows his father, I was wrong.

All of this is a basic denial of the reality of the situation. There will be something that will either gradually or abruptly make you aware of the gravity of the accusation. In my case it was the police coming to my home with a search warrant. That was an abrupt awakening. I immediately understood what could happen to me. I had been denying the accusation since I first heard it in August. By February the police were in my house. For six months I denied that this could happen. When it did happen a new emotion took hold – fear. That was my motivation to get started on my defense.

Fear: Most of the fear you experience will come from the unknown. You will not know what is happening on the other side. You don't know what people are thinking about you. You do not know what is going to happen to you. You will hope and pray for the best but you will fear the worst. I was accused of child sexual abuse. The father of the children in my case was a police officer. My greatest fear was that a prison sentence was really a death sentence. What chance would I have in prison as a child sex offender of a cop's kid? Who would protect me? I used that fear as motivation. I understood I was the victim of a mentally unstable mother who wanted me dead. I began to analyze the statements of the mother and child (in their interviews with authorities) and I found many discrepancies. I also worked on every aspect of my case. The fear of what could happen to me opened my eyes to the reality of the situation. I conquered my fear by working feverishly on my case.

I also had some fears that seem frivolous now as I look back. I was afraid to go near a school during the time the children were going to or were being dismissed. I was afraid to go any place where kids were such as Disney World. I was afraid anytime I saw a police car. I was afraid anytime I saw someone I didn't know on my street. I watched cars that parked near my home to make sure the people in the car got out and went into a house. These feelings were not only based on fear but on shame as well.

Shame: The sad part of this experience is that even though you are innocent you will feel shame. My wife's sister is the grandmother of the children in my case. She is a nurse in the maternity ward where my grandson was born after my trial and acquittal. When my son and his wife came in the front door of the maternity ward to have their baby my sister-in-law ran out the back door and did not return to work until they left the hospital three days later. When my wife and I came to the hospital we hesitated going into the maternity ward because we were worried what the other nurses thought of us. Not only did we know I was innocent but when my granddaughter was born my trial had taken place several months before and I had been found not guilty. Despite this we still felt several moments of shame. The accusation of child sexual abuse will stay with you your entire life no matter the outcome. You and your family will have to become very self-confident and not be concerned what others think of you.

The other sad part of shame is the child. In cases of false accusations the child has not been abused. But because of the perverted motivation of an adult or the system the child will believe they have been abused. The oldest child in my case went to a psychologist once a week for four months despite the fact that the psychologist said no abuse was found. The system then sent the child to therapy forty-two times, to a place where abuse has to be confirmed before being seen, even though no abuse was confirmed. Because of these sessions the child can create memories that don't exist and now feels the shame of being sexually abused. In my opinion, the caregivers and authorities who contribute to this are guilty of abuse themselves.

Guilt: You are innocent of any wrong doing so you should not feel any guilt. There will be times when you reflect on your life and past actions. You will look for something you did or did not do that caused these false accusations. You may also look at those close to you. You may blame yourself for the pain and suffering they are going through. I kept asking myself, what did I do? What did I say? Even today I feel guilt. My wife and her sister will never speak to each other again. I sometimes wonder if it is my fault. My son was laid off from his job at a city connected agency and I wonder if it was my fault. I have to stop and remind myself that my family and I were the victims. It is natural for you to want to take responsibility for your actions. Don't look for blame where blame does not exist.

CHAPTER 9

Dangerous Emotions and Feelings

There are feelings and emotions that can adversely affect your actions and your health. They may also have an adverse effect on your family and friends actions and health. The dangerous emotions and feelings during this ordeal are: depression, hatred, anger, pain, despair, stress and disgust. There will be times where you can be overwhelmed by your emotions and feelings. It is the loneliest feeling in the world. In the darkest moments of my ordeal I felt alone and helpless. I had thoughts I never imagined I would have. There were also times where it was difficult for me to function. There were days I took off work and there were days I looked for an escape. The weight of the accusation made me tired and weak. It sometimes took days for me to review documents related to my case because of the emotional stress. I had to learn to deal with and handle these emotions and feelings. To some degree you will experience a part or all of these emotions and feelings. That's OK. You need to understand what is happening to you emotionally and deal with it. Letting your emotions and feeling adversely affect you will get in the way of proving your innocence. There are also times when your family and friends are adversely affected too.

Many times the child, the accuser and the falsely accused are members of the same family. There will be grandparents, aunts and uncles, brothers and sisters, cousins, etc. Anger and hatred are probably feelings that will surface among family and friends. Some will hate the accused and some will hate the accuser. No matter what happens the family will be permanently divided forever. In the case of an adult making a false accusation they will need to recruit allies in establishing a case against you. This will cause more division and more emotional stress. You will be in the difficult position of dealing with your own problems as well as understanding and/or dealing with the emotions and feelings of your family and friends.

Depression: This is the most difficult feeling I had to deal with. Even though my ordeal is past and it had a favorable outcome for me I still think I suffer from bouts of depression. It did not take me long to understand I was depressed. I briefly thought about getting anti-depressants. I did not understand when it was happening but my brother was my cure for depression. He was the one person who studied and researched every aspect of my case as much as I did, if not more than I did. His daily calls brought me back to fighting mode and created a team feeling.

Almost every day I experienced feelings that I associated with depression. Sleeping was the part of my life most affected. There were nights I would just lay there and worry what was going to happen to me. I kept dreaming about the movie "Shawshank Redemption". I kept thinking of the helplessness and the hopelessness of being innocent and being sent to prison. How would I handle being in prison? The sadness of what would happen to my family. Many nights I just laid there almost crying. I can't tell you how many nights I laid there thinking about all of this and before I knew it, it was time to get up and go to work.

There were also days all I could do was sleep. Working on my case sometimes made me so tired. I had no energy and no interest in doing anything but just laying there and sleep. It was difficult for me to concentrate on what I had to do. I also had headaches and pain in different parts of my body. I can't tell you how many times I had back pain. Depression also affected my appetite. There were days I didn't eat at all and days that I ate everything in sight. I felt a need to escape my situation. My wife and I constantly took overnight trips to nearby casinos. I am sure that my wife was as depressed as I was and this was an escape for both of us.

There were times depression made me want to give up. Not to just give up the fight but I wanted to give up on life as well. The possibility I would be found guilty and sent to prison was almost too much for me to handle. I blamed myself for the pain and suffering my family would suffer. I am a longshoreman, which means I load and unload cargo ships. We work all hours of the day and night. There were three times I was working in the middle of the night when I thought seriously about ending it all. There were three nights when it was raining or snowing and I was alone on a container ship. All three times I was on a narrow walkway overlooking the hold of the ship with only a rope railing between me and the hold of the ship. When the hold is empty it is about seventy feet deep. I looked at the rope railing and the empty hold and I thought if I jumped down into the empty hold of the ship I could make it look like an accident. I even confided in two close friends that if something happened to me to make sure my family was taken care of.

All three times I was alone on the ship for several hours. On a container ship the crane does all the work. You are only there in case something happens where you need a man on deck. I was in such deep thought I was not even aware of the rain or snow. Each time I reviewed what was happening to me. I realized I was wallowing in self-pity. I also came to the conclusion my morality would not allow me to commit such an act. But most of all I came to understand this is not what my family wanted. I also became filled with anger and hatred for those who were doing this to me. I received information from discovery the first week of December. This all happened over a two week period after I received the information. The documents I received in discovery looked really bad and I did not know what to do. It was then that my brother saved me. He started breaking the information down and we started to prepare to fight back.

If you are falsely accused of child sexual abuse it will be a depressing event. You will suffer some level of depression. How far and how long you sink into depression is up to you. On one of our escape trips I bought a book at a rest stop that really helped me. The title of the book is "Have You Felt like Giving up Lately" by David Wilkerson. I thought it was fate I found such a book at a remote and unlikely place. The book is a spiritual book and I don't claim to be spiritual. The book gave spiritual answers but I also used the table of contents as a guide to find my own real life answers to my problems. The need for spiritual guidance is a personal choice. I was not looking for it and I kept it to myself but it did help me. It also helped me get to what I really needed to do. Get over my depression and get to work fighting for my freedom.

In order to conquer depression you must recognize you are suffering from it. From my research I have accumulated a list of warning signs:

- Sadness, anxiety, or "empty" feelings;
- Decreased energy, fatigue, being "slowed down";

- Loss of interest or pleasure in activities that were once enjoyed, including sex;

- Insomnia, oversleeping, or waking much earlier than usual;

- Loss of weight or appetite, or overeating and weight gain;

- Feelings of hopelessness and pessimism;

- Feelings of helplessness, guilt, and worthlessness;

- Thoughts of death or suicide, or suicide attempts;

- Difficulty concentrating, making decisions, or remembering;

- Restlessness, irritability or excessive crying;

- Chronic aches and pains or physical problems that do not respond to treatment.

Anger: This is an emotion that can cloud your judgment. It can also change your personality. You will become angry at the people who are a part of the false accusation against you. You cannot allow that anger to cause you to act irrationally. Nor can you let the anger get misdirected at someone on your side because you let your emotions build up. Focus your anger on those on the other side and don't let it affect the people who are supporting you.

Anger can also cause physical confrontations. In the course of everyday life the parties, their family and their friends may come into contact with each other. Child sexual abuse is an emotionally charged issue and it can be very easy for tempers to flair. My brother was at a convenience store and encountered the children's father. My brother had a few choice words about the children's mother and the father took offense. The father went to his car to get his gun. Fortunately, there were a lot of people there and the father backed off. This incident happened several months after my trial and there was still a lot of anger.

Do not allow anger to cloud your judgment. When I first started developing a defense I was angry and I hated everyone on the other side. In the beginning I believed the mother was crazy, the police were lying, the children were brainwashed, etc. My anger and hatred caused me to make accusations against everybody. You have to set aside your anger and logically disprove the case against you. Every time I read the reports and interviews in my case I became quite angry. I had to set aside my anger and logically analyze the data to prove my innocence. Many times I got up out of my chair and paced around the room because I was angry at what I was reading. That anger wasted my time. I was able to get a lot of work done when I put the anger aside.

Stress: The physical and mental effects of stress can be quite debilitating and devastating. Stress is different from your other emotions and feeling because it cannot only cause mental problems but physical one as well. Being falsely accused of child sexual abuse is certainly a stressful time.

I am not a medical doctor or a psychiatrist so I cannot diagnose stress but based on my research here are some of the symptoms: Aggression, Apathy, Guilt, Numbness, Headaches, Hot and Cold waves, Depression, Diarrhea, Sweating, Tingling, Nightmares, Bad mood, Tension, Inability to focus, Low self esteem, Hives, Sense of vomiting, Irritability, Disappointment, Loneliness, Speeded heartbeat, Being worried, Tiredness and Body Aches. I have also found stress can effect: the nervous system, the musculoskeletal system, the respiratory system, the cardiovascular system, the endocrine system, the gastrointestinal system, the reproductive system, the immune system.

The important thing to understand about all of this is that you are not the only one in this stressful situation. My parents were in their 70's when this was happening to me. I know stress had an effect on them as my father's health rapidly deteriorated. My oldest son, who was in his late 20s, went to the emergency room with chest pains close to my trial date. All tests indicated he was healthy and the pain was likely caused by stress. For some, existing medical conditions can get worse as the result of stress. There is no doubt you and others around you will suffer some physical effects. I don't really know how you can avoid it. I was stressed out when the police came to search my home. I was stressed out every time I visited my lawyer. I was stressed out when I had to turn myself in to the police to be officially charged. You will have to deal with stress in your own way and try to relieve the stress of those around your. Stress is an inevitable feeling and emotion of the process.

Despair: This is when you lose hope and confidence. There will be times when you doubt the outcome and your hope and confidence will be shaken. The most dangerous time to suffer from despair is when the District Attorney offers you a plea bargain. If you make a decision based on a feeling of hopelessness and lack of confidence you will regret it the rest of your life. Since you are innocent a plea bargain offer will be quite traumatic. My plea bargain offer from the DA was 2 to 4 years in prison and fifteen years of probation. If I was convicted I was facing a prison term of up to twenty-two years. By the time I received the DA's offer I had been working many months on my case. I knew I was innocent and I had the confidence I could win. If I had been in a state of despair at that time I may have accepted it to avoid a worst case scenario prison term. I would have given up two years of my life for a crime I did not commit. I would not have seen the birth of my first two grandchildren and I would have been placed on a list, branded forever as a child abuser.

CHAPTER 10

Seeking Legal Advice

If you haven't been charged but you know there are accusations out there that are directed towards you what should you do? My advice is to seek out a lawyer for a consultation. Many lawyers will offer a free consultation or an hourly rate to advise you of your rights. Make sure you understand your rights and that you have the right lawyer before you commit. Don't be pressured into turning over a large retainer right away.

Choosing the right lawyer is the most important decision you will make during this whole process. You need to objectively look at your options. It can be difficult even knowing where to begin finding one. If you have an existing relationship or friendship with a lawyer do not ask them to represent you by default. You need a lawyer who specializes and has experience in this area. My friend is a lawyer, I initially asked him for help. He recognized he did not have the experience to represent me so he contacted several law firms he was familiar with to find the best lawyer in this area.

If you don't know a lawyer who can help you find the right counsel you can begin with searching the internet and your local bar referral program. I would advise against using a public defendant. You are fighting for your life. In my opinion public defenders are overworked and do not always have the resources to be able to give your case the attention it demands. You need to choose the right lawyer for your situation; if you are assigned one by the system you are taking a risk.

When you find a lawyer you are considering retaining to represent you set up an interview. Ask your prospective attorney general and specific questions. Are you comfortable with the responses the lawyer gives and the manner in which they give them? Do they believe in your innocence and are they willing to fight hard and to the end for you? How often will they meet with you during the process to discuss the defense? Are they overly confident they will get you off or are they being honest and explaining the realities of the difficulties ahead of you?

You should be confident in the lawyer you select through the whole process. If your lawyer becomes unresponsive to you or otherwise demonstrates some incompetence to mount an aggressive defense do not be afraid to change lawyers. Innocent people go to jail because of poor defenses mounted by incompetent lawyers. Never let your fear make decisions for you. Get the best defense you can.

CHAPTER 11

Preliminary Trial

If you are not familiar with the inner workings of the legal system, a preliminary trial will catch you off guard. It is not a trial where you will be found guilty or not guilty. Its purpose is to determine if there is enough evidence against you to justify going to criminal trial or if the case should be dismissed.

Now that you are at the preliminary trial this is the first time you will likely be able to piece together the origination of the accusations as you will get more details than ever before. You will begin to identify who the parties are involved in the investigation and prosecution of the case, not just the alleged victims. The DAs, child services, therapists, DHS among others.

This is where I learned about the chain of events that got the authorities involved in my case. It started when DHS was called by the mother stating the children had been to a psychologist. DHS called a local child advocacy group. The Child Advocacy Group called the police. What I was unaware of at the time was that my city was one of the cities that used the MDT. At the preliminary hearing I learned those three entities were present at the interview. The police did not conduct the interview, it was conducted by the Child Advocacy Group. The information gathered from the parents and children's interviews was then discussed by the three groups once a month along with the district attorney.

The arrest and/or search warrant are the only place you will see evidence or accusations against you prior to the preliminary trial. Those charges will be sketchy and incomplete. In my case, the search and arrest warrants listed only the statutes which I was accused of violating. They did not list specifics of the evidence that led them to believe I had committed those crimes. In those documents, they do not have to list all the charges that will eventually be brought against you. This combination of missing evidence and incomplete charges makes it very difficult to develop a defense until the preliminary trial is underway and you become entitled to discovery.

At the preliminary hearing the DA will present the full list of charges to the judge. You need to prepare yourself and your family for a shock because the situation is about to get worse. Initially, when you learn about the allegations you'll see a few charges against you. For me, in the warrants only 4 charges were listed for 1 child. At the preliminary hearing I was charged with 22 charges for 2 children making the total charges 44. I was blindsided as I did not expect more charges, let alone the other child to be listed. The judge may or may not dismiss some or all of these charges at this point based on the current evidence. The DA knows this which is why they will charge you with as much as possible hoping that most of them are allowed by the judge and they can proceed to criminal trial.

It is difficult to know what to look for in the preliminary hearing to discredit witnesses or evidence. Because you will have little knowledge of what is happening. In my case for example, I learned the children went to a psychologist for four months. The psychologist did not believe any abuse took place. There was no physical evidence so it comes down to the psychologist or interviewers opinion. The mother and the MDT chose to ignore that professional's opinion and continued to press forward. This is the type of information you will not have prior to the hearing.

You will start to hear new terms such as hearsay, which is inadmissible in court. Hearsay is testimony based on what the witness has heard from a third party. Not something they experienced first-hand. Also, testimony presented at the preliminary can be carried through to your criminal trial. The youngest child testified I did not do anything abusive to him. However, six months later at the trial he testified I did abuse him. Because the testimony carried through to trial my lawyer was able to discredit the youngest child's testimony.

As I progressed through my preliminary hearing listening to the testimony, learning how the court worked, and meeting all the people and seeing the evidence I found it very intimidating. Outside the courtroom I had a defiant attitude. Inside the courtroom however, I felt threatened and there was a very real possibility I could go to jail despite my innocence. I desperately wanted to get up in court and try and proclaim my innocence. But it is important to adhere to the system and trust in your lawyer.

One of the most personally difficult facets of the preliminary is that it will likely be the first time you see your accusers in person since this all began. The children, parents, family and friends who have are pursuing your conviction will be there. Some of them you may not have realized were against you. Not only will you be facing the other side. So will the people who have sided with and supported you. This can be an intense situation for your supporters who may be seeing, for the first time since this began, family or close friends who want you to go to prison. My wife was looking at her sister and nephews. My kids were looking at their aunt and cousins. All though tensions may be high, it is critical that you and everyone with you stay calm and refrain from any physical or verbal altercations or outbursts. A judge or jury will be looking at the people present and evaluating them along with all other evidence and testimony.

Another difficult thing you will have to deal with is how to address the alleged victims and witnesses. I was aware the judge would be observing my facial expressions and body language. I was unsure how to look at the alleged victims. Should I be sympathetic, cold, upset? You should discuss this with your lawyer. In my situation, I kept my eyes intensely on any witnesses that testified against me.

In my case, the oldest child said I did not abuse him or see him without his clothes on. The DA asked him if I ever took pictures of him. He said yes, which was enough for the judge to allow my case to proceed to criminal trial.

Discovery is supposed to happen within 10 days of the conclusion of the preliminary hearing. Discovery is when all the evidence is given to the lawyers involved so they can properly prepare a defense. In my case, my preliminary hearing was in the beginning of September. I did not receive any evidence against me until December. It was stonewalled by the DA, which I later learned was a common practice. In fact, the stonewalling continued right up until my criminal trial when the judge entered the courtroom. We stood and the DA finally handed my lawyer a paper with a timeframe when they believed the abuse took place.

Chapter 12

Criminal Trial and Expungment Hearing

At my trial there was no physiological report or physical evidence. Both boys stated I had done nothing to them in sworn testimony. Other witness's testimony was inconsistent and contradictory. In all my trial only lasted 43 minutes which is virtually unheard of. Ultimately, the judge's verdict was not guilty. The DA simply didn't have any evidence against me. The process of getting to trial from the first accusation took years, cost me tens of thousands of dollars and was an emotional roller coaster like I've never experienced before.

The actual criminal trial was the briefest but most agonizing part of the ordeal for me. My lawyer and I had prepped for months to be ready. I had contributed hundreds of hours of research breaking down statements from witness interviews looking for inconsistencies or contradictions with the help of my brother. My lawyer did a fantastic job of discrediting witnesses on the stand and the DA failed to prove any charges let alone any charges beyond a reasonable doubt which was their burden to prove.

My trial was very unusual in how quickly it ended when it finally began. It was the exception, not the rule. You should prepare for a longer, drawn out trial. The DA did not have any evidence against me, the witnesses were not credible and the judge had many reasons to have a reasonable doubt.

Despite a not guilty verdict the system will remain persistent as it did for me in finding you guilty. To illustrate this point I am going to move on to the expungement hearing which took place months later. The expungement process is the final step in clearing my name. I was found not guilty months earlier but I still had to apply to the state to remove the charges from my record and to be removed from a child protective list which I was placed on when the charges were filed. In many cases this is a formality. Sometimes it is done by the lawyer and sometimes you have to appear before the judge. In my case I appeared before the judge twice.

It is important for you to learn from the beginning of your ordeal what I learned at the end of mine. And that is most of the time no matter what happens family members, friends, DA's, police, social workers, forensic interviewers etc. will always believe you are guilty. In fact, they have believed you are guilty from the very beginning. Because of this you must learn from the start who you can trust and who you cannot.

When my expungement hearing took place my wife and I arrived early. One of the police officers involved in my case was in the waiting room so we decided to wait down the hall. A short time later the children's parents and grandmother (my wife's sister) showed up. When we saw them my wife and I decided to move to the waiting room. As we passed them my wife's sister tried to show her papers and said these are to help you protect your grandkids. My wife refused the papers. The children's father aggressively went after my wife cursing and threatening her. The children's mother stood there confused. My wife's sister stepped in front of my nephew to intervene. The police officer had moved to the doorway and he watched the whole incident. I believe if my nephew had not been stopped by his mother the officer would have allowed my nephew to attack my wife. This would be consistent with the police attitude toward me and my family through the whole process. The judge heard the incident and came out to the hall and told us all to come in.

I was amazed at this whole incident. It showed me that the family still believed I was guilty and they hated me more than ever. I thought they would believe their own children who had testified I had done nothing to them. Instead I found out later that they blamed the judge at my trial for my not guilty verdict.

When my expungement began the DA was different from the one at my criminal trial. The first argument he presented was to allow the children to testify. The DA argued his position for an hour. Our position was that the children's testimony at the trial was sufficient. After much arguing the judge agreed with our position. It was very confusing to me as to why they wanted the children to testify. Later, I realized they needed the children to testify so they could contradict their testimony at the trial if they had any hope of preventing my expungement from being successful.

The District Attorney began to introduce evidence. He had two pictures that were supposedly drawn by the oldest child which were used at my criminal trial. The DA had them mislabeled which in the context of the testimony made them more incriminating. My lawyer caught the switch and was able to have them reordered. The DA later tried to have them switched back again to the way he first presented them. The judge denied him.

All of the DA's witnesses were present except for the Child Advocacy interviewer who although subpoenaed chose to go to jury duty instead. Although the judge was not happy about this we proceeded with the witnesses that were present. One of the police officers was the next to testify. I was really anxious to hear him testify because I had filed a lawsuit in federal court against the police and others involved in the case. At my criminal trial he testified he and another officer had witnessed the interview of the oldest child by a forensic interviewer. At the expungement hearing the officer testified the other officer was never in the room to witness the interview and that he left the interview after five minutes. This meant that no police officers witnessed the interview of the oldest child. This testimony contradicted various warrants and official documents used against me. The police were willing to falsify affidavits for warrants and official documents in order to get a conviction. The truth was of no concern to the police. There only concern was getting an arrest and conviction on their record and in their mind getting a guilty predator of the street. Another disturbing abuse of power from the police that was exposed at my expungement was the police used a photo lineup that consisted of the driver's license photo of me and my two sons. This type of lineup is a violation of federal law and if the children had not pointed to me and pointed to one of the other photos then one of my sons would have been implicated as well.

My nephew was the next to testify. He really had nothing new to offer but you could see the hate in his eyes. I stared at him the whole time he testified and he never really looked at me. His wife was made to look foolish when she testified at my trial. So she was not called as a witness at my expungement hearing. I couldn't help think though how hate had overcome my nephew so much that he couldn't listen to his own children.

When we returned for the second expungement hearing the DA again tried to switch the drawings presented

85

as evidence with no success. The events that unfolded at my expungement hearings showed me the authorities and accusers will fight until the very end to destroy your life in any way possible. You need to be equally dedicated to fighting against them.

CHAPTER 13

What You Can Do

It is impossible to analyze every jurisdiction, agency or person involved in a case of a false child sexual abuse situation. I can only tell you from my experience and research what I believe should happen. You will have to take this information and see if applies to your case. If you find information you can use you should personalize it to your case. When you do that you can better fit the pieces into your defense. Just because you think something does not pertain to your situation you still may be able to adapt it in another way in defending your case. One thing I did at all hearings and trial was to buy a copy of the official transcript. I highly recommend doing so you can study the testimony to look for mistakes, errors or lies that you can use to prove your innocence.

Your lawyer will have a final decision whether something is to be used. If your lawyer rejects your idea make sure your attorney gives you an explanation. The legal system is complex and difficult for a lay person to understand. By asking your lawyer questions you will begin to better understand the legal system. It may help you in your search for information so you can contribute to your defense.

I gave my lawyer countless suggestions and information. If you do this make sure you have them organized and ready to present. An attorney's time is precious and you don't want to waste time with your lawyer on items you are not going to use.

My attorney focused in on two of my suggestions and my breakdown of the children's interview: I believe my first suggestion was what ultimately resulted in a not guilty verdict. During the preliminary hearing I noticed when the children were being questioned before they would answer they would hesitate and look into the audience before they would answer. It looked to me as if they were being coached. I suggested to my lawyer to make a request for the family and friends be removed from the courtroom during the trial. The following is an excerpt from my court transcript. I have taken the attorneys name out:

The Court: *"Very well. We're recalling the matter of the State versus Harrison"*

"Mr. Harrison has been colloquied. A formal arraignment is waived, a plea of not guilty is entered, mutual sequestration is ordered."

"Anybody who is going to testify for either side of this case is to leave the courtroom now and remain outside until the call of the crier. Anybody who is going to testify."

"Counsel take responsibility for who ever is sitting there."

Defense Attorney: *"I am right now"*

The Court: All right *"State you may proceed"*

District Attorney: *"He's already been colloquied"*

The Court: *"Yes, he's been colloquied. We're ready to go"*

District Attorney: "Thank *you. State calls (The Child)"*

Defense Attorney: *"Your honor, if I may, before the child comes out"*

The Court: *"Yes"*

Defense Attorney: "Since *the State is calling (Child's Name)"*

District Attorney: *"Yes"*

Defense Attorney: *"What I would like to ask your honor is that the courtroom be cleared, sequestration for the two minor children when they testify."*

The Court: *"What?"*

Defense Attorney: *"I would ask that sequestration –"*

The Court: *"Well, I have already ordered that anybody who is going to testify is to leave the courtroom"*

Defense Attorney: *"I'd ask that all individuals be out of the room so that there's no influence of the children looking around the room for different people to have any kind of interference with their testimony."*

District Attorney; *"Your Honor, the only issue that I would ask is that you're going to be sitting there and you're going to be able to view the child."*

The Court: Right. *"That's denied"*

Defense Attorney: *"That's fine your Honor"*

The Court: *"Let's get your first witness"*

> *"But I would caution anyone in the room that they are not in any way gesture, look in any way. And if I observe that, you'll be ordered out of the courtroom immediately."*

Defense Attorney: *"Thank you Your Honor"*

District Attorney: *"Your Honor, I would ask if I could just stand in front since it's a pretty large courtroom"*

The Court: *"Sure"*

In this exchange you may not be sure if I won or lost. I think I won. The D.A. was put on the defensive. The thought was put in the judge's mind that the child possibly coached. And anyone who could have possibly influenced the children during their testimony understood they were being watched. What doesn't come across in the transcript is that when the D.A. asked to stand in front the judge motioned her to my side of the room. The child denied all the accusations and I believe I was proven right. There was a tremendous risk in doing this. After months of research and review I was convinced the children were coached. My lawyer explained the risk to me and it was my choice to take a chance. If the child had testified differently the verdict could have been much different.

You must understand, just because you know something is true or right does not mean you should use it. I know the mother at the very least has deep emotional problems and probably mental problems. My attorney agreed with me about the mother's mental state. But he would not and could not bring it up in court because we had no proof. He was able to use the knowledge of the mother's mental state to discredit her in cross examination by asking questions that provoked her to the point where she was flustered and made mistakes in her testimony.

The second suggestion my lawyer accepted regarded the questioning of the child to determine his competency. The forensic interviewer, the assistant district attorneys in my preliminary hearing and my trial all questioned the children to test their competency. They wanted to know if the child was competent to give a yes or no answer. They never explained to the children what to do if they did not know an answer or what to do if a question required more than a yes or no. There are studies that show what can happen when a child is being questioned by an authority figure or someone they respect. In that situation when they do not know the answer they will make up an answer that they think will please the interviewer.

These two suggestions I made to my lawyer are personalized to my case. I knew the relationship the children had with several of their family members who would be present in the court room. From intense research and personal observation I came to the conclusion that the children were coached. The second suggestion I never got to use in court. On the stand, the child denied all charges so there was no need to question the interview.

The strategy was simple. There are three basic answers to any question: "yes", "no" or "I don't know". A "yes" answer is usually followed up with additional questions. A "no" answer means exactly that "no". In court an "I don't know" answer is usually treated as a "no" answer depending on the Judge. In my case the judge ruled that "if he doesn't know he doesn't know". In the interviews in my case when the children said "I don't know" they were pressed for an answer and then came the leading questions. I broke down the interview based on countless hours on research on protocols for interviewing children. You may be able to this yourself, you may need a professional or your lawyer to breakdown the interview. However it gets done you need to analyze the interview and look for flaws. If there is no physical evidence the interview will probably be the main reason you are going through this ordeal.

Chapter 14

What Can I Do (Part 2)

Since you are innocent the child's statements are completely false, coached, manipulated, influenced by leading questions, etc. The interview in my case was not audio or video taped. This made it more difficult to breakdown because I could not hear the tone of the questions or see things like body language. There is more to an interview than just questions and answers. There is the setting, the circumstances, the interviewer and more.

The first thing you should look for is the motives of the parties involved. The interviewer has to be unbiased to conduct an objective interview. The interviewer and the other parties involved, such as the observers, should not have an outside interest or ulterior motive. The purpose of the interview is to find out the truth about the events in question so the results will support a fair decision making process in the criminal and child welfare systems. The CAC did the forensic interview in my case. On their website, they stated they could provide the child and the caregiver therapy even before they come in for a meeting. The oldest child in my case was being interviewed starting at 4 P.M. The mother was being interview at the same time by the police. During the course of the child's interview the mother was told her child would be sent to therapy through the

CPA.

The child was sent to an agency that requires sexual abuse to be confirmed in order to receive therapy. He went to 42 sessions. The forensic interviewer knew before the interview was conducted that the child was going to be sent to therapy even though abuse was not confirmed. In my opinion, that is a conflict of interest and in my opinion the interviewer had to find sexual abuse to justify the therapy. I also found that the amount of cases handled has a direct effect on the federal grant money received. This showed me that the multidisciplinary team may have a conflict of interest. The more cases they had the more money they made.

The interviewer should also be testing the child's statements. The interviewer and the observers need to find out if there is another explanation for the child's story. For example; the oldest child stated I had chased him with a knife and fork. The police and the D.A. took it as abusing the child. They never considered an alternate explanation which was I was cooking and chased him out of the kitchen so he wouldn't get burnt while I had the utensils in my hand.

In order to test the validity of the child's statements the backgrounds of the parties involved should be checked. The parents in my case were taken at their word. There was no check for a history of abuse. There was no check for mental problems. The child was not checked out. The interviewer and the observers need to have complete information in order to make an informed decision about your case. In my case, the police did not even investigate to see if the child was at my home and in my care during the time in question. Without complete information the investigation will become biased and skewed in favor of the accuser.

The accuracy of the statements made by the child should be tested too. In the oldest child's interview he stated one of the incidents happened at 2 A.M. in the morning in August. The child was 4 ½ when this allegedly happened and he was being interviewed 1 ½ years later. It is very unlikely that a child that age will remember a specific date and time. During the interview the child should have been tested to see if he could determine specific dates and times. The child also reported my wife was in the bed at the same time and she was never question about the incident. The investigators accepted the child's statement and they never investigate a questionable statement made by the child.

The interviewer should also avoid asking leading questions or suggesting events. There are specific sets of protocols that are to be used during a child's interview. Every one of them instructs the interviewer to avoid leading question and suggesting events. If there is a way to find out what protocol the interviewer is using it could be helpful to you in analyzing the interview. If an interviewer does this they are injecting an adult interpretation into the interview. A child's wording and interpretation of an event can be much different than an adult's.

An interviewer has to stay on the child's level. When the interviewer injects their own thoughts or suggestions they may be above the level of the child. What is worse is the child may become confused. There are two possibilities. The incident never happened or someone else did something to the child. By asking leading question or making suggestions the child will probably be confused. Anything can happen then. In my case, the child made up implausible events such as pouring hot sauce on him in the kitchen. When the interviewer was asked in court what protocol she used she stated that the CPA had developed their own protocol. The interviewer must adhere to an approved protocol otherwise there is a possibility the interview will be tainted.

There are several things the interviewer and the decision makers need to know to be sure the interview is conducted fairly and objectively. Naturally they need to know the child's age, sex, interest and their development level. There are outside influences that could affect the outcome of the interview that need to be investigated before the child is interviewed. At the very least they should be checked out during the course of the investigation. Here is a list of things I believe should be done.

- **Immediate Family:** Are the parents still married? Have the parents ever been divorced or separated? Are there problems in the child's home? What kind of environment is the child's home?

- **Custody Arrangements:** It did not apply in my case, but I have read that many false accusations stem from custody battles. If that is true for you, be sure to check the time you had custody and match it to the alleged times of the accusation.

- **Character of Family Members and Friends:** I discussed the character of the family involved in my case earlier. You need to look at your situation and analyze potential witnesses for character flaws that can be used against them to help prove your innocence.

- **Child's terminology**: A child's vocabulary is not as developed as an adult's. They may use words incorrectly to express themselves. In my case started with the child saying he had been in bad pictures taken in a small room next to a big room. The mother assumed it was the bathroom in my basement. My kids referred to the basement as dad's basement. My nephews referred to it as Uncle A's basement and their children referred to it as Uncle A's basement. My friends even referred to it as A's basement.

97

I spend almost all my time in my basement. It is the main room for everyone in our house with people constantly going in and out. I have all I need there and no one refers to my basement as a big room. As young as the child was he still would have called it Uncle A's basement. He would not have called it a big room.

- **Frequent Medical Care**: I know the child was taken to the hospital for falling out of bed. I do not know if he had been taken other times. Frequent medical visits can be a sign of abuse. That is something you will have to find out in your case. The children in my case were taken to a psychologist. The authorities ignored medical history. The mother in my case did have a suicide attempt and was taken to the hospital and then referred to a mental hospital.

- **Outside Influences**: The children involved with the accusation had access to unblocked adult cable content. The father kept Playboy magazines in the only bathroom. They had older cousins who could have talked about adult situations in their presence. An outside influence can have an effect on a false accusation. It may not start the accusation but it can help to embellish it.

- **Suggestive Habits**: The mother in my case took showers with her two sons. I am not a psychologist so I will not interpret this. I will say that I believe this is not normal and it opens the door to several possible scenarios that could have influence the false accusation against me.

- **Investigate Possible Misunderstandings**: A child's words or actions can be misinterpreted. In my opinion, the authorities have a duty to the child and all other parties involved to investigate the possibility of a misunderstanding. They can do this by talking to all parties involved. In my case, once I got a lawyer the police and the D.A. had no interest in talking to me. Many times the authorities would rather expose the child, the accused, the family and friends to the damaging and expensive ordeal of a criminal and civil investigation and trial rather that speak to all parties and clear up any misunderstanding.

- **Investigate the Possibility of a False Accusation**: False accusations in child sex abuse cases are becoming more prevalent. The first responsibility of the authorities should be to be sure a crime has been committed. Many times though the authorities completely ignore the possibility of a false accusation.

The authorities have the responsibility to reduce possible trauma to the child and ensure fairness to the accused. An objective and unbiased interview is a major tool in these objectives. The preparation and follow-up of the interview can be just as important as the interview.

Chapter 15

A Look Back

It was and still is my opinion that any person, agency or municipal department should be held accountable for any misconduct in the investigation and prosecution of any criminal case. At the end of my trial even though I was found not guilty I did not feel vindicated. In the preparation of my defense I had found many instances of misconduct. Misconduct during the course of your case can be intentional. It can also be the result of indifference, ignorance, improper procedure, improper protocols or poor training. For my own peace of mind and for the protection of other innocent people who may face the same ordeal I did file a civil lawsuit in federal court. I also thought I would be protecting innocent children from the trauma of a sexual abuse investigation.

When I filed my lawsuit I felt very confident I would at least be heard. I had hard evidence. I even had court testimony proving my claims. There were several motions to dismiss and I responded to each motion. The Judge agreed with me on some points and dismissed some of the lawsuit. Then out of the blue I received a letter from the judge that my suit was dismissed.

After I got over the disappointment of having my

suit being dismissed, I started to think about what it meant. I had learned during the course of the suit that the DA and the police do enjoy some prosecutorial immunity. The judge had ruled I had overcome some of that immunity in my responses. My lawyer told me we were OK because the judge had ruled in my favor in most of my responses to the defendant's motions. Then without warning the judge dismissed my case without explanation.

The only conclusion I could come to was that the judge was protecting the system. I now understood that investigators and prosecutors are not held accountable for their actions. They can do or say what they want without fear. This creates a dangerous situation for an innocent person. By dismissing the case without explanation the judge is approving their actions.

The system has major flaws. You're job right now is not to fight the system. You need to work the system to prove your innocence. You will need all of your energy for the battle ahead. Be diligent, question the evidence and take the allegations very seriously. You won't have a second chance to get it right. I truly hope this book helps keep innocent people out of prison. No one deserves to be falsely accused and I hope you are one of the success stories. Good luck and get to work.

Manufactured by Amazon.ca
Bolton, ON

25676349R00057